One to Another

Roberta Hamer

ISBN 979-8-88943-333-0 (paperback)
ISBN 979-8-88943-334-7 (digital)

Christian Faith Publishing
832 Park Avenue
Meadville, PA 16335
www.christianfaithpublishing.com

Printed in the United States of America

Let me tell you about a love story, when it happened, how it became sad, how it became in helping one to another. I hope in reading this book, it will give you inspiration that you can overcome life itself.

'I can do all things through Christ which strengtheneth me' (Philippians 4:13).

One foggy morning, September 19, 2000, starting my day for work in a doctor's office. I was living with my parents. I told my mother to have a good day, while my father had already left for work.

Getting in my car, I proceeded on the way to work. It was very foggy that morning, listening to gospel music. Yes, it was traffic. Cars had slowed down for the stoplight. I was next in line to make the light after a truck that was in front of me. I didn't make my turn.

This was when it all happened. I had an accident; I heard a big crash. When it happened, I vaguely remember. I was slumped over in the car. I could hear people talking. People were coming to my car, asking if I was okay. I was out of it. I do remember saying I could not move my legs; both of my legs were pinned into the seat. To whoever was the first person that was at the car.

I remember the person asking me, "Do you believe in God?"

I said, "Yes."

"You are going to be okay."

We began to intercede in prayer, and all I could say was *Jesus, Jesus, Jesus*, and the person stayed with me. Someone called my mother, but that person stayed next door to my parents. When my mother came, both of them begun to still pray. My mother is a praying women and still praying as of today. That person that stayed with me, until mother got there, I can say that was my guardian angel.

Until this day, I don't know who this person was that stood by me, but I thank *God* for them. The paramedics finally came, they started talking to me, and they were putting the neck support around my neck, asking me if I was hurting anywhere. I told them I couldn't move my legs. Both my legs were pinned back to the seat. They were saying to me that they were going to try to straighten my legs to get me out of the car so they could get me on the stretcher.

That was excruciating pain for them to get me moved. After getting me in the ambulance, they started an IV, and they were giving me *morphine for the pain. I think I took all the morphine they had. My left leg was swelling by the minute.* They got me to the *emergency room* at *Wake Medical Center.* They began to work on me—doctor, nurses, and the ER tech. They asked me a question, "Is anyone out in the waiting area?"

Still asking questions, the ER tech had to cut my clothes off to put on my gown, take off my jewelry. I was in an out of conscious while the tech asking me more questions.

I was thinking to myself, *Why is he asking me all those questions?*

I was wondering what was wrong with my legs. He was saying to me that he would let my family know in the area what was going on with me. I told him to get my mother and to tell her to get in touch with my daughter. She was in college at the time.

The orthopedic doctor came in. He had to reset the bones in my left leg; they wanted to do that while I was awake. Working in the medical field, I told them to put me to sleep, reset the bones, and wake me be back up. Only my legs were injured, nothing else.

The doctor wanted to get some X-ray. The tech rolled me to X-ray and my legs were swelling by the minute.

While the X-ray tech was getting ready to slide me on that hard table, I was in so much pain, and I didn't want them to touch my legs. I wanted them to leave me alone. But they had to get it done. While they were getting X-ray, I was saying, "Jesus, Jesus."

The orthopedic doctor wanted to talk to my family and told them that my lower extremities were badly broken, especially my left leg, and that they wanted to amputate my left leg because it was broken in so my places. My right leg and ankle were broken as well, but not as bad.

My mother, my father, and I said, "Do not amputate my leg. Do what you have to do to save my leg."

In the meanwhile, the ER tech had to get me ready for surgery, along with the nurse. The ER tech had to remove the polish off my fingernails and toes, still letting my family know what was going on with me. They rolled me down to surgery, and it took six to seven hours before they were done.

I finally got up to my room, and I was still groggy. I heard voices—my parents, my daughter made it from college, my nieces, nephews, and friends. After the nurses got me situated, everyone was there. My family went to get something to eat and my dad stayed because my mother was bringing him something back.

I remember asking my dad, "Do I *still have my legs* because *I could not feel them?" He said yes.* I began to *pray* to *God,* "*Thank you, Jesus.*"

My left leg had eight screws sticking out the top of my leg, also a screw going through the side of my left knee, two screws inside of my left foot. My right leg had two screws sticking out the side of my leg. Three screws in my right ankle. The journey had begun.

The next day the doctors came in to make their rounds. They were touching my legs and ankles, as if I was not in pain, it hurt. They were doing their job. After that the hospital staff started coming in every three hours. Screws were in both of my legs, and there was so much blood on the bandages.

The very same day, the physical therapist came. The nurse wanted me to stand up to put weight on my foot but the pain was unbearable. They had to lift me up to put me in the chair.

As the weeks passed, I had a lot of visitors, and my family stayed overnight in the hospital with me, which was a blessing. I really appreciated that. I do remember asking someone about the *car,* and their responds was the front of the car looked like a pancake, but the funny thing was that the windshield of the car was just a straight line going across.

I said, "*But God*, I am *a miracle child. I could have lost my life. Thank God.*"

The doctors, still coming in to check on me, sent me to X-ray to see how my legs were healing. I had to have another surgery on my left leg. This time, I had something I called HALO by the screw going through my left knee, six pens sticking around out from my knee, with a rod connected so it could stay in place.

The ER tech still was keeping an eye on me. I was wondering why he was doing that. I was trying to get well. I had to go to rehabilitation to learn how to walk again. That was another journey. I didn't want to go, but I had to, still asking God to get me through this.

The song by Yolanda Adams, "In the Midst of It All," I listened to that song every day. Even when I went home, that song is what brought me through, nobody by *God*.

I got to the rehabilitation center, and they rolled me to the room. I told them I didn't want to stay in that room, the reason being, the other patient didn't like to be cold. It was like an oven in there. I asked to put me in another room, so they did. They had to get some more help to move me to the bed. The lady that had my foot, I didn't think she knew what she was doing. She had not done that kind of work before. I screamed it was very painfully.

I said, "I didn't want her help."

My daughter came down from college the same day. I was glad to see her come. I got emotional because I didn't want to be there. She put her arms around me, and said you can do this, you are strong, you will get through this. That made me feel better.

In my career in healthcare, I have worked in assisted living and rehab facilities, who would have thought I would a patient.

The ER tech was still coming to see me while I was in rehab. The people were so nice to me, even though they were working. They would pop their heads in to see me. The social worker, physical therapists, and nursing assistants.

Some days I felt like giving up, but I kept saying a prayer, asking *God* to keep giving me strength each day, so I could keep pressing my way to strengthen my legs and to stand and take steps, and God did it.

My parents came to see me when I was in physical therapy, and they had a smile on their faces. I had so many visitors that came to see me, people from my church, friends, and the ER tech. They were still praying for me. I thank God because that is what brought me through, during the four months there, and it was hard. *But, God*, I was able to go home, back to my parent's home.

I was still in a wheelchair, and I still had screws in my lower extremities. The screws (fixators) had to stay in my lower extremity for another two months. I was unable to walk or to do anything for almost three years. I still had to go to physical ther-apy to learn how to walk again and how to stand. I don't know how many times I cried because I was so independent, but I couldn't do anything for myself. I had to wait for someone to come.

Everyone took me to therapy, even the ER tech, he was always there to help out. He came when my parents had to do errands. It was Christmas time, and he asked my parents if he could take me to see the Christmas lights. I was thinking to myself, *How are you going to get me in your car?*

Believe it or not, he picked me up out of the wheelchair, carried me, and sat me in the seat. I asked him if I was heavy, and he said no. He was laughing when he said that. I was happy.

I was in a wheelchair, but I graduated from a wheelchair to a walker, then a cane. With *God*, he will do it.

As time went by, he continued to come and visit me, even when he got off work on the weekends. We even went to the movie theater. He took me to see his cousins and his family and told them that I was going to be his wife.

Here I go again thinking to myself, *What is he talking about?* I just laughed.

He asked me to marry him. It took me a while to say *yes*, but I did. He asked my dad if he could marry me. It was some question, but he got through it. My dad said yes.

That day came, and we were married. He was still doing things for me. Just say we were there for each other. We traveled, went fishing, and just had fun. He even taught me how to put a fishing worm on the hook. He told me if I wanted to fish, I had to learn. I just laughed, but I did it.

We enjoyed going to church. My husband became a deacon in the church we attended. He operated the sound in the church and called him the Sound Man. He didn't mind helping people.

Throughout the six years we were married, he developed a rare form of cancer. He didn't want to tell me. He talked to our pastor first, then he told me. He said he didn't want to upset me. We went to appointments after appointments. The doctor told us my husband had to take chemo and radiation, but that was not what we wanted to hear.

Through it all, my husband was still pushing himself to still try to work, until he couldn't do it anymore. But we were still praying. He was in and out of the hospital, and he was in a rehab facility, until one day, I went to see him, and I didn't like the way they were treating him. I brought him home, and I said to myself with *God's help*, we will make it. He was there for me when I was down, and I am going to be there for him.

Yes, it was hard. Trying to work four hours a day, but thank God there was help. One of the church members came in and stayed with me through it all. Someone was coming in for two hours to assist my husband. Everyone was coming in to visit. His mother and some of his family and friends came to visit him.

The pastor and his mother made a tape of some songs that he loved, and I played it every day for him. It was until my husband got worse, and he had to go back to the hospital. The doctors said there was nothing else they could do but to make him comfortable. It was hard to see him lying in the hospital like that, but *God* kept giving me strength.

I was preparing myself as to when that day will come. I stayed in the room with him, and when I went home, someone else came. I was asleep in bed and received the call that my husband had passed. My daughter and fiancé met me out to the hospital. Again it was so hard, my friend, my husband was not here with me anymore, but *God* brought me through, with my mother, church, family and friends praying for me.

This is my story. You never know who may come into your life, whether it may be good or bad, that person may be there for you through it all, no matter what the circumstance are. You can make it, in helping each other. Watch when you get on your feet, later they might get sick. Until this day, I may have a limp when I walk,,but I am still her thanking God each and every day. It could have been the other way. I return the favor, my husband was there for me, and I was there for him, *one to another.*

Therefore encourage one another and build
each other up, just as in fact you are doing."
1 Thessalonians 5:11

I hope as you read this book, it will
inspire someone. You can make it.

The End

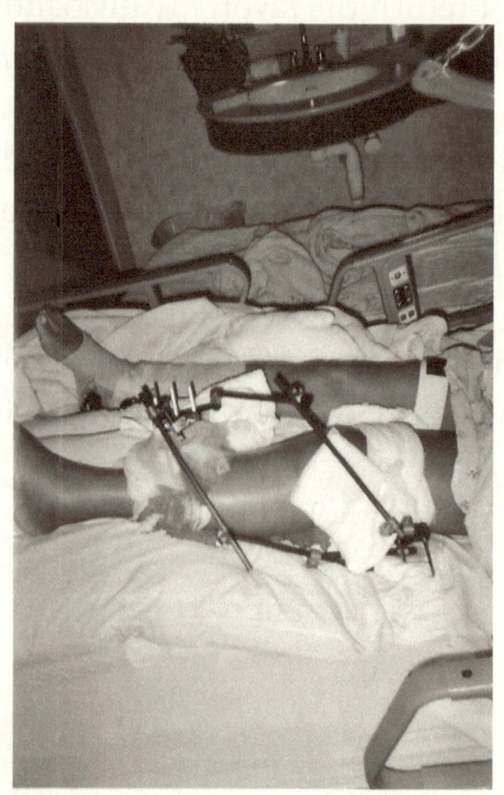

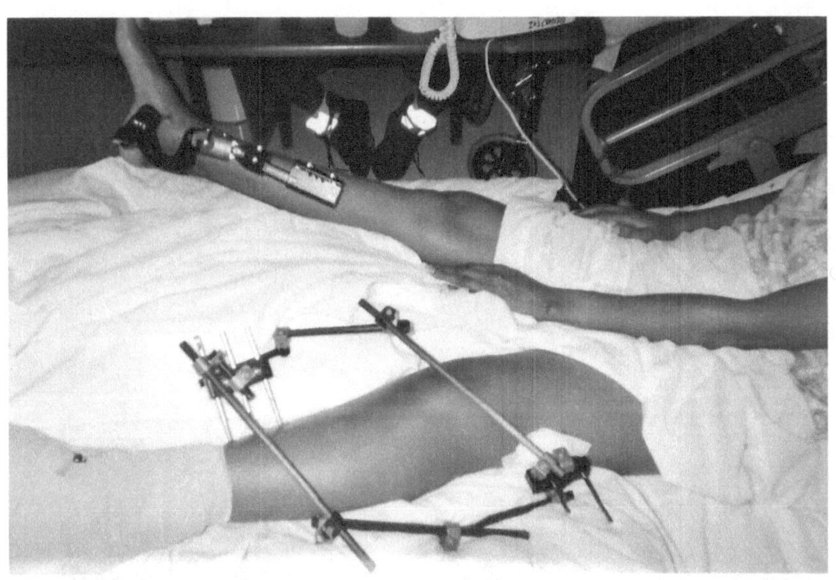

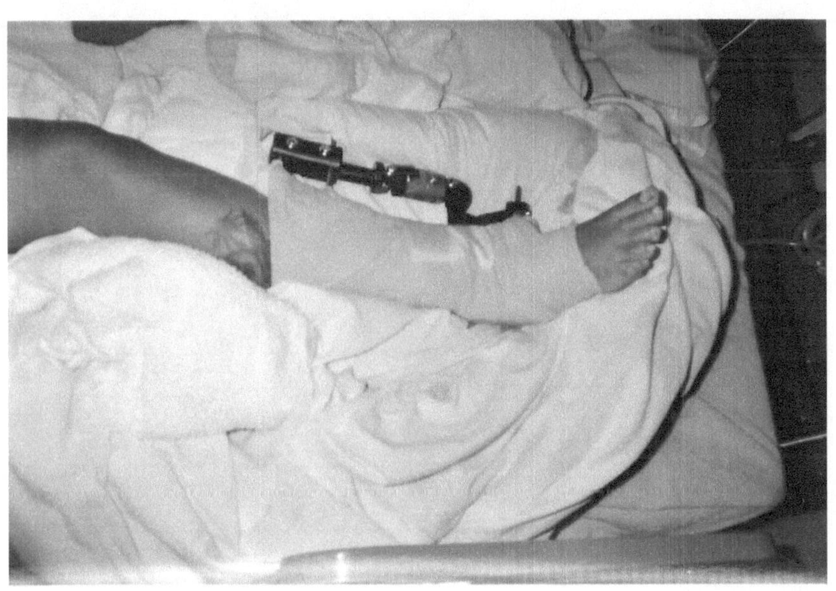

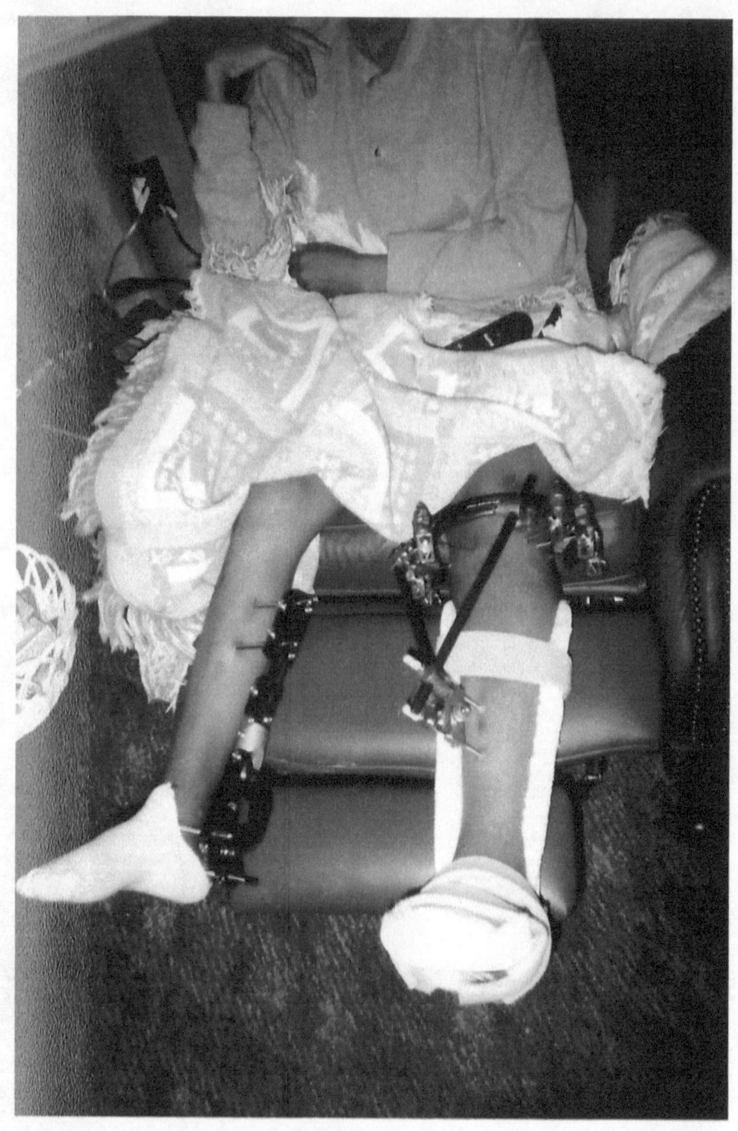

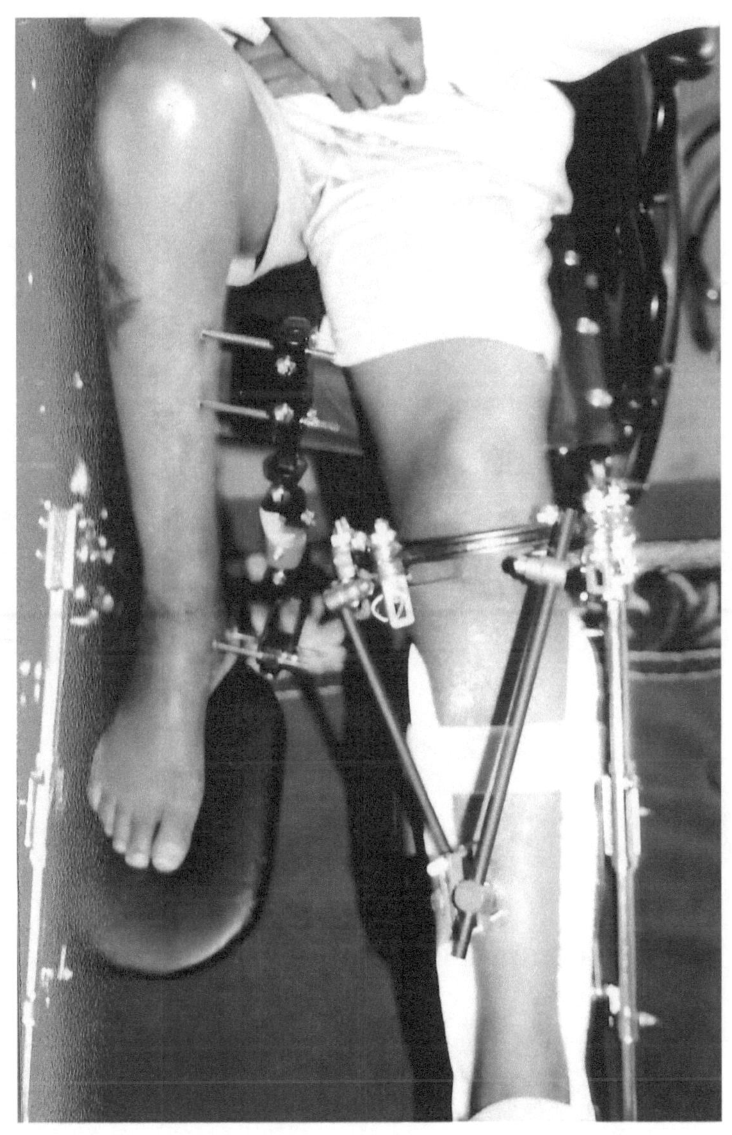

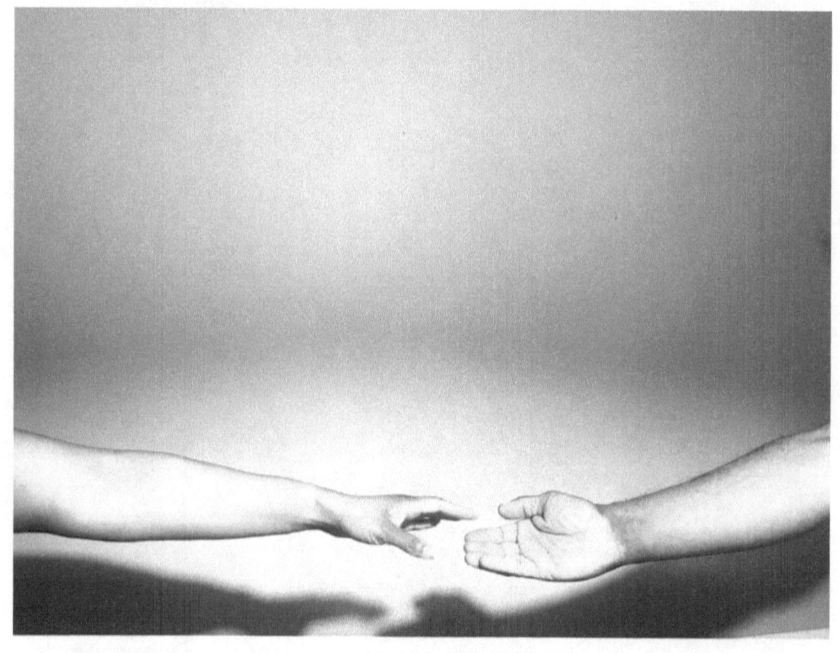

Everlasting hands can never be broken

ROBERTA HAMER,
AUTHOR OF ONE TO ANOTHER

Roberta Hamer native of Raleigh North Carolina, I am the last one of the family out of seven siblings, they say I was spoil, but I don't think I was. After the accident, which happen the year 2000. I started writing this book. This is my First book that I am writing, hoping that it will inspire someone. I was married to my husband for almost six years, we were both in the medical field of work. I enjoy helping people, and to be an inspirational to other, spending time with family, and granddaughters.